Forest with Castanets

This book is manufactured in the United States of America and printed on acid-free paper.

Library of Congress Cataloging-in-Publication Data

Names: Mehta, Diane, author.
Title: Forest with castanets / Diane Mehta.
Description: New York, NY : Four Way Books, [2019]
Identifiers: LCCN 2018028830 | ISBN 9781945588259 (pbk. : alk. paper)
Classification: LCC PS3613.E4257 F67 2019 | DDC 818/.609--dc23
LC record available at https://lccn.loc.gov/2018028830

Four Way Books is a not-for-profit literary press. We are grateful for the assistance we receive from individual donors, public arts agencies, and private foundations.

This publication is made possible with public funds from the New York State Council on the Arts, a state agency,

and with funds from the Jerome Foundation.

PROUD MEMBER

We are a proud member of the Community of Literary Magazines and Presses.

Forest with Castanets

Diane Mehta

Four Way Books
Tribeca

This book is dedicated to the history of my feisty, restless, see-saw spirit. And with extreme love and appreciation to my son Ivan and my father Dilip.

"That's the trouble, because everything on earth is a riddle."
The Brothers Karamazov, Dostoevsky.

Contents

Morning of the Monsoon

Blue-black weather sizzles when it smacks the asphalt.
Ocean air tumbles in, loosely shaped in networks of water.

Embroidered marigolds on muslin, canary-yellow kurtas,
pelican-pink blur together in the wash
flowing in rivulets down the grooves of roads

the British built. Rainwater aimless as worshippers
tilted in prayer, chanting the old rhythms.

The monsoon works itself north. Cashews infuse the air
which thrives on motion, ripe fruit, and daily appeals—
a step up in the next world, more love.

Defiant, clouds gather, then fling down an annual sum:
12,000 by flood, 289 by riots, the rest burned to the bone

with garlands. Ash is the color of the road,
my grandmother's ashes cold as my mother's bones,
remains that will be mine. Words don't last in me—

there are too many dialects. I tilt into finite.
The rest plug into a circular, scene-shifting pull of souls—

Nirvana and the rest, *rapture*—
to be cut loose from life, its repetitions hell.
Like walking into the shade.

Immortal Stories

In this city of crows and rose-ringed parakeets,
elephants and camels labor down the beach,
marionettes tell stories in knotted banyan trees.
Old monkeys with young men, men-monkeys in old stories
more pure than whatever we believe.
For a half-century I wandered the Hanging Gardens
where one farmer and topiary animals are stuck in their cosmology.
Monsoons blow by, the dead disintegrate and find new lives.
Still they hold their shapes.
The topiary farmer will never plow his field.
He treadwheels the same triangular plot of grass
tilling the same immortal land
under cloudless skies or fat rains.
He has witnessed new irrigation and exports of tea,
arrivals of King George and Queen Mary
for which the water's edge jetty
blossomed into the basalt arch that is,
for ordinary souls, the Gateway of India.
The farmer has listened quietly as millworkers
lurched from red-light rooms to wives
spreading love. He has seen famine and plenty,
the arrival of antibiotics, the purge of syphilis.
He has agitated for self-rule in his photosynthesis heart,
he has marched with his plow

in demonstrations from the start.
He has seen the blood-burst of Partition.
He is destined to be cut and trimmed
again. So much for love, he thinks, it is not here
any more than I am.
He is doing the work of life, he will never reach Nirvana
though he will pray forever.
A peacock calls the operatic light
in a field behind the two-acre forest our gardener built
near the shanties that rose under the palm trees and skyscrapers
that Nehru built. I am sailing to my old Bombay
of my oldest dreams, into my aunt's cosmos so antique
it resembles neither the beginning or end of time
only the building blocks of matter
where principles of motion and rest are divine,
which brings us to the topiary man and his plow
pressing infinitely on.
There is a light show in the fountain in the evenings.
The farmer feels all four seasons on his hedge-skin
as if teasing him to join the human feelings.
The field needs tending, he says, eyes lowered,
and leans into his plow.
I retreat as sundown lifts over the hill.
Oh what promise this passport permits.

I am no longer lovely.

People chatter on in more dialects than I remember.

I am visiting my old home on the fifth floor

with its salt-sea view and terrace of my parakeets.

Up the street the topiary man is still plowing and plowing his field.

Tropics

I

Once, in those mirrors of Indian sunlight,
Talking mythologies, Arjuna in his field
On the distant edge of my experience.

A blue-hot, companionable wind
Heated the land. It did what tropics couldn't.

I took what I was entitled to—
Comic book abstractions of the epics,
Its vivid illustrations. Reading was when we felt
Most deeply, princes returning from a war
To children raised in wild woods.

We took our destiny with common sense.
A child was just a child and not some future thing.
Love was closer to a pastime: cricket, tag, a swim.

And yet the slower pitch of what we knew
Back then was too enraptured, barely true.

2

In ex-colonial hills, we rode the tired horses
And chased down Fords beaming to a halt.
Lights like fireflies in sticky evergreens.

Ooty: between the commerce of the Raj
And slopes scented with tea and eucalyptus.

Roads sewn like perfect little seams
Into the green Nilgiri mountains.
Azure trains cross ancient wooden bridges.
The way to India is on the haunches
Of what the British built: rose gardens and bonsai,
Diesel locomotives, St. Stephen's church.

We looked for pebbles on the hills,
Tiny silver sequins on the vast, unfettered growth
That held its leaves up to infinity.

And never were so proud. Mountains like charms.
Blue smoke slept with us through sunrise.

3

Pretty swastikas embroidered into textiles.
For your doorway, they said.
(Not a charm for Jews.) And then my mother left.

In truth, they were right angles, arms bent
Back to antiquity. Tantric force and good health.

Marks of spirit-lives, say ancient scribes,
Wealth if you want it.
Above a door, auspicious entry—
Symbols to live by: a cross, a *hamsa* amulet.
Her search for Jewish time was keenly felt.

Still, she remembered the math. The grid, the hard
Calculations of philosophy at home among tiny prayers
Angled to God in Jewish pews.

A synagogue with Indian smells, songs lilting
Into ceremony and Hebrew blessings.

4

Blue as a peacock's chest, my bicycle had three speeds.
Down the paved path from the canteen
I pedaled up the hill towards the susurrating sea.

The air was riven by unidentifiable bird calls.
Green-feathered trees argued with bougainvillea.

On a rope tied to a life buoy and attached to a servant
Without one, I bobbed deliriously on icy waves
Imagining unicorns or sprites, all tugging the tether—
Magic beyond, dangerous mermaids
With iridescent tails living second and third lives.

We held on tight against the possibilities—
Berserk tears, breaking sun, summers not gold-glazed.
Japan beckoned with watery, salt-black syllables.

The West was purple-blue, the sun brimmed over—
Our parents' eyes were soulful as they watched us swim.

5

The country was rife with prayer.
Slokas, chants, a muezzin's call, an offering.
Avatar-sating coconuts, the excitement of garlands.

We worshipped in sunlight synagogues,
Peeked in altars, saw effigies of Ganesh get sea-swept.

Faith was what you celebrated, not ideas themselves,
As if belief were just a proof, an everyday calculation
Of rightness and karma, good deeds that rise from acts.
We put our love in contracts. We read our Bibles, Koran,
Pentateuch, and *Mahabharata,* and believed each one.

Yet what we listened to was underneath drunk love
Of gods or god, above the ritual that gives it structure.
It hummed between ancient spaces in our words.

I don't know anything. I believe what parents authorize.
Prayer is in our hands, it just shows up.

6

We were sunlight in 24 karat, ears needle-punched.
We swam in Breach Candy's oceanside-designed blue pools,
Peopled with foreigners and half-whites.

Yet we loved it; the terrifying high dive
From which we flung ourselves like temporary angels.

Women slid by in strange bikinis, men in lounge chairs
Listened to the sea. A fuller education than philosophies
Swarming in temples, shrines marigold-brightened.
We untangle our desires among a Jain backbeat of denial.
Nirvana, to child-eyes, was the lost and found of India.

We swam farther down into chlorine-clean depths.
Below the sparkling surface, if you looked up,
You could see the lifeguards stand in their seats.

Total immersion is heaven-sent. It was steps to the sea;
We peered over, its tidal provocations splashing our feet.

7

The humidity soaked our faces in the blur.
Monsoon settled. Our gardener bloomed the terrace.
Pencil trees and frangipani-scented paths we wandered.

I knew even then kindness was sewn
Into people. However you feel it.

I've found some darkly hazy truths, some fiction
But nothing I care too much about untangling.
Better to be briefly amazed
This is what love is. More a maze of moments
Than fact in fine print, lists of things.

Parents flow into us like sugar and medicine.
We let them go a little
But not because we will it.

The sea murmurs its salt-drunk secrets
Like ancient families drifting with me.

8

We were one generation behind the bungalows;
Corinthian columned villas and cool tile roofs
Razed to earth for high-rise nationalism, for *Jai Hind*—

Free India from 200 years of power—
Roads, rail, arms, cotton, law, books, electricity.

Yet still: *satyagraha*, Gandhi's passive resistance
Soulfully exchanged beauty I longed for in photographs,
Mixed society that half-resembled me.
I'm a Jain-Jew mutt from India and yet American—
Not empire, ex-pat, tribal, not any country's citizen.

The city of a thousand common lineages is faith-swept.
Reincarnation fills it with candle-bright faces,
Puja-giving souls bent at the altars of homemade temples.

My temple lives in the sea, with memories and bare feet.
Its gifts are cold water, its only worshipper is me.

9

Beyond my bamboo terrace, between home and blue—
Sea salt shimmering on my tongue, places to float to,
Myths and devils and international questions.

Sun-up sounds arrive: *adhan* from minarets,
My grandmother's a cappella Jain trilling.

I want what is least Indian: more love.
Heads are bent in thousands of temples
With sweeter prayers than I am capable,
More time than I have stored in Jewish bones,
Another cosmology with its souls of kindness.

We are astonishingly blessed.
Faith that is not dreams, not church, not love;
It is palpable, fully developed, without commotion.

The shelter of ritual disappears in the daily heat.
I am a chimera, an incongruous Greek myth.

10

America was all exuberance. Land of evergreens
Snow-dusted, its splash of silver seas and more pools
Than we could swim in. Gleam of the new eternal.

Children grinned through Hindi when they heard.
Teachers looked hopeful. America the compassionate.

I sang my America of Christian hymns looking west
With my Christmas songbook. I smelled the Arabian Sea.
A cousin country, both English, but by pronunciation
Utterly unlike: India was a dactyl, all force, and America
Two iambs, as if saying, we are always back and forth.

I yearn to be one continent but I am not; I am all force,
Swimming in two seas, hiking Everest at 30,000 feet.
I am on the Brooklyn Bridge but perpendicular to it.

Landscape of palms and seasonal oaks,
My America is half blessed, halfway to exuberance.

Ears to Magic

I took the scene and ran with it,
diaphanous from outside in and darkly wondering.

How was it that the light just kept diminishing,
my tropics-exultation a charm hot days rang in.

What empty wilds I wandered in,
thinking with my feet, ready to live in it.

I put my ears to magic, all delight,
slipped into cutouts between shadows.

And hoped to learn, from inside out, something—
that I am sunlight-bound, incomprehensible.

I came from the east, resinous and sun-melted,
thinking all souls are one day heaven-smoked.

Yet here is a land of normal caskets, a place
for stone biographies, a miniature place.

There are too many answers. Hard facts
are carved on headstones from tiny faces—

Not the faces of India but my Jewish deficits
doused with the eternal light I never wanted.

I don't mind it, these fir-needles, wild-scented
nothing, my exit-entering, my heart in two countries.

Mythical Underground Above the Street

Hauntings steam up from sun-soaked pavements,
rogue roads I rough-trod for 30 years
where my footfalls met the footprints of my soul
ridiculously raving.

Yesterday, I stole it back
with fox-like thrills.

I hover close above my shadow now,
my feet fall into step.
I spin myths of peacefulness
but shatter tender beats along the streets.

I lived beneath the ground
which all along was shifting.

Elephantine roots and fat ferns adorned the path back up.
Gigantic skies refracted so much light
the world seemed reconstructed
but it was only accurate.

Each year slakes its thirst on eternities
blossoming inside it.

Leaves palm-up in prayer, that scientific light!
Seasons grow old with it. It rises up
as I descend, its emancipated sensings
rooted in old-growth realities true as my two feet.

Groomed Water Descending in Prisms

Darkening thunder of foghorns—
smoke-saturated thirst of gypsies posing as oracles.
A downpour's blind beat peppers our skin.
Roulette clouds and the wild wind,
we are lost in it. A train rumbles at the same pitch
at which the storm sermonizes and we believe what we find
we believe. The natural world maneuvers the bends—
all that groomed water descends in prisms.
In your eyes are optical tricks: silhouettes and rain-shine,
this angle or another. Sounds of real life
hooked in their corner of time
rewind, a sea squall miles out
unseasonably rages. I take from it the flying tires
and four-door birds, certain I know
less than before. Still in the mix: turning corners
that don't exist, spirit-animating X-rays.
Brick dwellings have lost their outlines
and light has turned to blur, but is less uneven.
My passionate resistance, thank god,
keenly falters. I am soaked to the skin, you are out of earshot.
Proof of all we might have been
is the light-separating lens of a prism,

your gaze in it. This maze is beachfront,

streets lead out from the ocean the same way they approach.

All things function in tandem,

even the pavement against which rain ricochets.

Elegy: A Jewish Death

I

My moon-walking mother flies sideways in the yard.
Black fences spike and spiral to contain her.

I race to find her half notes tilting
into the delicate tide of Chopin's *Berceuse*.

Orchestral agitations take to air—
punched out phrasings, dark timbre of violins.

She floats blood-red in a yellow dress
with lace-webbed wings she'd never have chosen.

That was my part but now I'm no longer certain.
I stake my heart on the hopeful trauma of D major.

She shadows me, a rococo menorah,
arms holding prayers up, pulling light around me.

2

I praise the gentle luminescence
though I can hardly breathe.

Little insurrections in my bones and in the trees.
Possibilities skitter to my feet.

I paper through the Torah for blue breezes
but find a zodiac and yellow fever, parched vistas.

Can I find what I cannot feel
in its enchanted translation?

I turn to the synagogue of maples,
their gently rejoicing leaves.

Branches are labyrinths. Primitive doubles of me
pray in languages I cannot read.

Spikes of delicate branches corral light
in decline. I sink into nightfall.

The eternal light yields more people
out of reach: phrases in soil, rustle of trees.

Arms of evergreens clutch at sky all year,
the pale blue gentle enough to breathe.

3

Limbo comes with daylight at six.
She exits my longing, shifts

like the sea at dawn into simpler
things I'd like to believe will find me later.

She will find me later
among the greater

intentions, in moments of believing
she is closer when I'm grieving.

I listen in silence to her sounds,
it shakes my soul to the ground.

The hours are fixed, eclipsed
by her circumference.

The Jewish element looks for the Gestapo
in the shade, the rogue

wrong-impressions I cannot
evade fast enough, times I ought

not to have thought so much
about love; it was enough.

It is certain she will find me later,
I will meet her in the black paper

among the undulations
of ancient conversations,

among the rhythms of light on the sea
glittering, and she is with me.

4

Tumbling clouds, fear of bliss or blessings
too religious, amassing then drifting apart

as if the long-dead read our thoughts
and expertly judge whether we cherish enough

and whether we mark our time with blood
to sniff out better love. Not in this graveyard.

Shade moves weirdly to the right
across three tombs on the western incline of the sky

in this third year of mourning since she died.
Grass has overgrown the dirt,

the skyline seems afloat.
In this green abode for names and bones

her laughter brims over
flowers, branches, fence, grass, stone

as if my being there had built momentum
for the kind of afterlife

she lucked into: full of great disasters
and personalities to decipher.

5

Unveiling

So I have taken up the colors of the sun
in anticipation of her place, slightly insane,
in the ground-breeze beneath the shade of a tree,
where seasons halt and people are free
to talk about oranges or big ideas
undone on canvas, or which madness escaped
the things it most believed
quickest. Shrewd, shucked of fears,
her mind glimmered. Among shade-shapes
on the stone there inscribed: I believe
says Maimonides. Amazed, I stand in disbelief
and watch a thousand commotions seem
suddenly normal, her way of seeing
sideways into the obvious. Sideways now is she.

Remember You Must Die

Books of the dead are useful for the living. The ancient Egyptian book of the dead, a catch-all term for all kinds of illustrated funeral texts, functions as a guide, with spells, to help get you to the next life. They were written on the walls of burial chambers or on coffins. Buddhism has a book that bridges the afterlife; the Tibetan Book of the Dead appears to have some useful tips, such as how to transfer your consciousness at the moment of dying. (You are on your way to enlightenment.) If not, you suffer the fate of living again, that cyclical existence from which Hindus and Jains want *moksha*, or deliverance. Dante, of course, similarly tackles the soul's trek through the Christian afterlife. Only Judaism has a book of life, though it exists in concept only, not on the page. It occupies the same mental space as death books in how it confronts repentance. It's said that on Yom Kippur, the Day of Atonement, God decides who has properly repented for their sins, then writes and seals those names in the book of life. It comes from Exodus chapter 32, verse 32, which, in the King James edition of the Bible, says, "Yet now, if thou wilt forgive their sin—: and if not, blot me, I pray thee, out of thy book which I have written." God blots the sinners out of the book.

Are we righteous or are we not? Just as in Jainism, the religion of my father, Judaism also requires us to be accountable. Setting aside the various cosmologies and what you get in response to living a good life, the structure of this religious concept is poignant because it gives us occasion to reflect.

Several months before my mother died, she told her health care aide about a dream in which she was asked to sign her name in a big book.

"What does it mean," she asked the woman, knowing very well, I'm certain, what it meant. It's probably no coincidence that she was Jewish and was signing a book of life, a recognition that she had reached a point of forgiveness and ease—past suffering, humiliation, and dementia. The book of life, like the books of death, records the fact that *yes*, you lived. It is also a bookish kind of cemetery in advance of the real one.

When we buried our mother, I looked around to see who her plot was next to. There were my grandparents, their names etched in the tombstones. I looked around at the Jewish names in every direction, the tree my mother would be under, and appreciated the shade and shape of it. My mother drew trees in charcoal for many years. Here was her tree of life above her freshly new life of death. The terms become interchangeable. What is a cemetery if not a book of death? Tombstones record some aspect of people: whether they died young and whether they had children, whether they were housewives or whether they had professions.

"This graveyard is a kind of evidence that other people exist," says an elderly woman in Muriel Spark's *Memento Mori*, looking back on middle age at the time she walked through a graveyard and stooped to read the names on the tombstones. Names are not unimportant. In her biography of Jane Franklin, the sister of Ben Franklin, the historian Jill Lepore uses Jane's book of the dead to reconstruct her life. This incredibly smart, uneducated, married-with-a-dozen-children woman lacked the opportunities that her prolific brother had. All she produced was this sixteen-page book, or pamphlet, a list of dates and names of family members who died. Lepore makes much of the book and its timeline, for it recorded the people around whom Jane's life revolved.

Hindus also have a book of death. They take the departed's ashes (known as "flowers") to religious towns around the Ganges, where priests keep books on generations of every Hindu family. The family priest performs a ceremony and then asks the family to sign the book of death before he pours the departed's ashes into the river. When a priest records a death, he also records new additions to the family, such as babies or children-in-law. The records go back hundreds of years. When my father's friend Kris's father-in-law died, he and his wife went to a town called Haridwar ("God's door") to see her family priest. When Kris found his own family priest, he discovered that the priest was computerizing his records and had taken it upon himself to add the cause of death, a modernization that the priest hoped would help predict hereditary illnesses. Of course, you cough up money for this: Death is not free.

When my dad had his sixth stroke, I asked my sister for our mother's book of books. She had kept a journal, since 1974, of the 481 books she had read between 1974 and probably the mid-eighties. She didn't produce much. She had some essays and articles she had written early on in her marriage, a sheaf of letters she sent to her parents from Europe, recipes she collected or which she typed and scribbled notes on from her time living in India, and her book of books.

I scanned the list of books with admiration. It starts with *Last of the Just*, a novel about Jewish persecution in England, and ends with Susan Cheever's biography of her father. She read a ton of Bernard Malamud, Saul Bellow, Stefan Zweig, Graham Greene, John Cheever, James Dickey, Joan Didion, Yasunari Kawabata, Jean Rhys, Pär Lagerkvist, and everything by Thomas Mann. And there were the Brontë sisters and Jane Austen, whom I remember her rediscovering in her fifties. In between the literary fiction was evidence of confusion: *Women & Anxiety*, *The Wonderful Crisis of Middle Age*, *The Will to Live*, *What to Do with the Rest of Your Life*, *Alternatives to Teaching*. Countless books on back pain fill in the blanks. Lists tell a story. It's clear what kind of writer she would have been, if she had put her mind to it. Her description, at seventeen, of seeing England from a steamer for the first time, in a letter, was akin to the excitement she expressed to me in a letter during my first trip to Europe, when I was eighteen. Her fifty pages of letters were full of elation. My mother documented the things that had made life bearable despite her health problems and her many varieties of despair. She may not have died in a dignified way, but that doesn't matter.

Sherwin Nuland, the author of *How We Die*, says that just as we are unique in life, we are each unique in how we die. But what's curious to me is the ways in which we are not. We die in a variety of ways, but we unravel in ways that are much the same. Dying badly is simply the nature of what kills you, he said. My mother died an anguished death, miserable nearly to the end. For a long time, I resented her for it. Why couldn't she have cleaned up a bit in the hospital? Unlike my father during his recent hospital stint, she was not stoic. On the other hand, she underwent years of pathological depression, terrible pain, heart disease, colitis, and the loss of most of her faculties. It took me a long time to recognize that I was the fool with respect to my mother's dying days. It was I who was undignified to assume that she should die the death that I admire according to the going rate: our collectively inadequate, cleaned-up version of our unraveling. "Death belongs to the dying and those who love them," Nuland said. You suffer and grieve, and good for you if it's not messy.

A Double Sort of Likeness

Companion poem to Martial, Book X, XLVII

Your life at rest, mom, is far more heavenly:

some peace, a temple, lightning, kindness, love;

benedictions for the soul, talk that nourishes.

An intimate bed; keener arrangements of tenderness;

marrow of bones and Russian books;

an autumn dacha in mushroom woods,

botanical mornings, with rose and eucalyptus;

evenings of gin-bliss and steady friends;

years to meet my son, to tell him strange tales

irresistibly grim, but tuneful, and not untrue;

more laughter, for now you are a decade dead

while sparrows rush up into the trees.

Pretended Homes

In the hummingbird woods where you believed me
And eucalyptus smelled like the future
We invented a bridge and walked to the middle
Where sky reflected in sea-green the tributaries
That blended oceans. We found rock libraries
Of antique books waiting to be spoken open;
Polish and Turkish flew in and landed on thin branches—
We traded *Street of Crocodiles* for *Snow.*
We invented a child utterly and invincible
As if counting what to expect. He questions us now.
Where are the facts? Where is dinner clanked on the table
Grooved with a thousand plates?
We hand him a list of declensions.
We exit rooms from opposite sides.
We read him Grimm's and say these are the tales of life.
These are the sounds you will wish to escape.
These are the clowns who smile through their teeth.
Here are the fast-bruising people with big feet.
And here the scene shifts.
Water sparkles as daylight burns off
Mist and condensation in the hummingbird woods
By the sea-green lake that feels like the ocean
You will find when you are older, with its tidal glories,
Its talking mermaids and brave sailors,

Its lung-tightening heartbeat.

We are still a family, we promise,

And prove we are parents

With love so disabled

It mimics a century-old translation.

Here is the pain of the books we traded,

Here is the new math you're learning;

You will grow into it later.

His sentences feel like essays;

There is so much buried in them.

He turns on the reader like an old man,

Not a third grader,

His accusations buried under spelling mistakes.

On the lake in the valley

Of the moss-soft marriage

We used up,

Fat snow drifts onto my face.

You are gathering wood to burn our sadness to.

I fall asleep without you,

Half-frozen on a hill on the Upper Hudson

By a small blue cabin.

Our son is with me.

Stars leak over the snow into moonlight,

Sky in cut glass, its silvery apprehensions gone,

Our marriage over.

I show our son pictures and give him music he cries to.

I watch the magic of Ophüls and Kusturica

And think I will never be

Anything but 50 percent in the beautiful gown

Our son keeps telling me to wear.

I have no body to fill it.

This, we tell our son, is marriage.

It is fluid-blue and grief is a routine.

Under the Volcano

Fanatical in knowledge, we are always losing.
Today I was fingerprinted, proved in the world.

Immediately the other part dwindled.
I was so empty, birds settled in me.

I walked down 3rd Street to the playground
without my son. A bluegrass band jangled.

He was with his father in his trapeze life—
split-house swing of moving platforms.

Every night I'm in-between here and Mexico
paining through Lowry's drunk-dense sentences.

The steady liquor of light, his blackouts,
burns back the married affections I cherished.

I mine my alphabet of comics, soil of dirt-sounds.
Chapters with fanciful ghosts I marvel into—

Gin-swooning confusions under *Popocatépetl,*
gutted with marriage-breakings. I miss my son.

Today, sun-saturated moments are elsewhere,
he in his father's arms, and I distantly entangled.

Unholy Sonnets

I

Street life scattered into broken nouns.
A quiet year unraveled in my hands
And lit the tiny spaces I walked into.
Sidewalks winced at shadows
Slanting through them. Daggers, I said,
And they agreed. Love seemed elsewhere.
But then I stopped to think. Well, was it?
Ancient skies said join us, come on up;
A thousand ears were listening from the clouds,
A gentle congregation. We garden here, they said.
I considered their eternity and shouted back, no thanks,
I'll take tough verbs and scattered daylight.
Chrysanthemum truths are not
What I am after, although they scent the world.

2

Rainlight and a storm increasing
Overhead. The day cascading into pieces,
Gowanus overflowing and the bridge is up.
No access to the bar I love, where two men
Mix drinks I guzzle with smoky nuts.
The clouds pull in. They batter my heart.
I am two miles away where lightning gets shaped,
Each flash handmade into something
That illuminates a darkened life within.
If I could find the grace to be that ghost,
To let myself be light-filled, I'd be all soul
And all transparency, for one moment
Unreasonably clear, a brain-stung
Electric Fury that has no way to hold the lightning in.

3

The cadence turned into a drumbeat.
No rest for skin-carved hours, my type O
Torqued into a clot; it bursts, it races
Naked, seeking peace, flows
Into my house-street, greenhouse, feet-house,
A backbeat-driven instrumental—
Old pain engorged with new feeling.
My breath tightens, then slacks,
Lacks everything I had accumulated.
My home implodes into my feet, air I breathe
Bloody. Down to the canal that cuts
Through Gowanus; the rut, the muck, the haze-drift
Settling onto the chemical surface of green water,
Clinging to my knuckles, knees, feet.

4

In the tender rationality of neighborhoods
Our sons are young (but they are shades).
We tune ourselves; summer of perpetual solstice.
Brooklyn seismically beats. Tag, soccer, barbecues
And our constructions. Sumptuous beliefs in things,
Leafy streets to wander safely in, our diminishments
Arrested. But shadows tilt in argument. Perpendicular
To rows of Norway maples, ginkgos, silver lindens,
Filth lines up in cans we hide our garbage in.
Sky brightens to blue, pulpit-trees say *believe*—
My smoking-alcoholic dream of sun-drenched Sundays
Turns incoherent. Light moves west. I'm a whiskey-tough
Junkie of new and newer love more lust-entrancing,
Less hideous than the last. My noose-tight empty street.

5

Giant cranes crank up in Red Hook, reflecting back
Unwieldy truths. They weep and rise again,
Task-driven and inconsolable.
We all arrive and leave on the same coast,
Cerveza and linen, bangles and bananas
Tossed back, far-fetched by winds that own us.
Our coastal siren-giants of industry
Sing *less weight, more love*—
If we could all be mermaid-wild within ourselves,
Unhinge grief. To stop unloading tiny dreams
Daily by the thousands, to toss each burden off—
But worlds on shore, their feet cemented.
Containers stack up like books with stories in them.
Foreign languages float in on schedule.

6

I am making our home at Green-Wood.
Among serious stories and serious ghosts,
In a fresh grave by a lake near young souls
Pondering their reflections, I am making our home.
You are asking the Steinways if you can fix their pianos
In a slanting valley under the shade of a tree.
I am walking the grounds, looking for unknown poets
But find knuckles and knees, soil-scented bones
Unperturbed by new arrivals or rhythms of weather.
Above us is a projection of our continuum together;
A thousand scenes of a thousand endings,
Catacombs beneath. We will bury our love there
For safekeeping, we will bury our love
And dig it up again.

7

Ravaged, unredeemable, I melt into my feet
Murderously myself. I long for peace but (admit it)
Laser cut and polish grief. My perishable universe.
Mythical forests everywhere but in these streets.
Machete fences hung with ears, spines, cheeks.
We consorted with torment and said it was beautiful.
A bruising daylight sparkles with vowel-defunct
Love, a bloody, shunted mix. I see everything now.
I am a zigzag of a woman loving
Our chain-tight tango of intimate deceptions.
Mirrors, Borges whispers, hold duplicates of me.
I am racing to find them. We are lottery-rigged.
We stone each other daily, skies our witness.
You record of disaster, you vision of underneath.

8

It seems medieval, the glow-fog of evening
Softening around lights slanting up to meet the drizzle.
A tall religious float sits waiting to be transferred.
Desolate night of primitive moments.
Black warehouses and the BQE ablaze with lights—
Trajectories we end up in. I am colored with weather.
I walk inside the stucco bar, quietly unraveling.
My friends converse in Balkan jazz with cool clarity
That seems to go on forever. Its truth beats chaos into me,
Their improvisations better than our rough rhythms.
I mourn our tuneful conversations, melodies torqued
Into bluegrass that moved too fast. Bliss-miserable,
I couldn't shake it out. I elide into lyrics only I can hear
And let my body jazz itself to peace without your cult.

9

Narrative disasters mapped on this fine street,
All fists and contraband and darkly radioactive.
I am undimensional, a silhouette of weeping.
Historic grief slopes down to meet me here in Brooklyn
In bitter embers with sea-chants of dead immigrants—
But I am high up in the breezes where nothing
Blossoms, arrested in steep grief. It is midnight
Again. I miss our stark sensations,
Our groves of oranges and eucalyptus
Inside where it is snowing and we are cast in darkness.
Was it even lovely or was it rapture ruptured?
My musings drag me down on this fine street.
What if every trouble is my every inspiration?
What if every trouble leads back to me?

10

Aftermath-erratic, longing for bright sensings—
New cadences I strut around with—
Gaelic, Aramaic, Latin, Old English
Waiting to be found. I reconsider my language:
Unmoored letters, growls and echoes
Scuffing up the muck of syntax
In these green acres where you are always quiet
Above my thundersweet acoustics.
There is no shame in weeping.
Half-notes, *arpeggio,* you beating me blue
In dissonant evenings, cravings arranged
To seem seductive. Around it I am eddying—
You hung me out on clothespins to the elements.
I spread my sleeves and let the weather in.

II

Summer's steam-heat glitters up the avenues
Around which Gowanus traffics. I jitter down
To the canal with my notebook of serious beliefs,
Looking for the clarity of fiction,
Not this free dive into the noir of losing.
Stink-sludge of perpetual drift,
Obsession its own high, which comes too easily.
We are entranced in grandiose affections,
Our rhythm mixed, no melody in it.
Wild-haired mornings jackknife back,
Skin-scents of wood dust and metal shavings,
Your sea-glass eyes watching—
I am enraptured with endorphins of my rage,
Rearranged, a dark unease lingering.

12

Indecisively fruitful: our thrilled scenes.
My eyes are in my feet.
Dragonfly wings glint in humid August;
I stroll into eternities handmade and impossible.
My disembodied shape is fog between concrete.
Summer drift. Is *this* what love is?
Through this one love, all other loves disintegrate.
My son is waiting and he misses me
While I linger in this darkening dazzle.
I argue to the death: It is my coffin to climb into.
So what if love roughs me over, so what
If love is nothing more than backbeat.
Criminally intent, I turn my silence up.

13

Our deepening surrender, so cloistered,
Anyway held an absence
Where a faint sound, spirited into being,
Drummed into a love-compounding beat
Repeating structure, our conceit.
Abbreviated spaces. I puzzle into
Ravishings of de Kooning, Reverdy, Donne—
Crepuscular twilight and its bewildering would soon
Desist, if new ravishings had old ways to be
Cajoled, loved, compelled into
Couplets, pauses, clashings, cymbal-smashing
Actualities. And then, in a flash of knowledge,
Repose. Undignified, I wouldn't find myself
So true to something, even, yes, an absence.

14

Swayed with the sauntering, fine-tuned ways
You fill a space that I am wandering in,
A prolongation of my life, so darkly cruel,
And pause, remembering our buoyant rendezvous.
My days are tentative, with wished-for glitter.
But I felt too much love; it's just a riff,
Too atmospheric, and I have lost all my realities.
Age will blast me out, bone-chilled, and to the hilt;
It yields what's true, what's blessed.
I lean into each day more carefully now.
Love was different, and then it felt no different
From the skidding awfulness, its tired lyrics.
Someone else's song is transposed on mine—
I no longer want it and the gambit's up.

15

Underneath, there was an ancient music
I underestimated so you could be *minus* and *post*
Romance in our soul of things trundling around
Old truths but not believing. Luck-seeking,
We pretended we were young, but we were only
Freak-making love-taking strangers
Shining up our contemplations, building new homes
Profoundly not our own. *Alone*, my trope, is this
Lingering over your major promises in minor chords,
Melodies short of lyrical. You are *un*listening.
I long for scenes more narrative, midnights less ravishing.
Art and its companion-tale, your skin-sentences
Shimmering and I, except you unravel me—
Shake the dark out, and shake myself free.

Sex & Sensibility

Vivian Gornick describes the journey to self-possession as one of unimaginable pain and loneliness. "It is the re-creation in women of the experiencing self that is the business of contemporary feminism: the absence of that self is the slave that must be squeezed out drop by drop," she says, quoting Chekhov, in "Toward a Definition of the Female Sensibility," from her 1978 collection *Essays in Feminism*.

The journey, Gornick observes, is "one in which the same inch of emotional ground must be fought for over and over again, alone and without allies, the only soldier in the army, the struggling self. But on the other side lies freedom: self-possession."

Last July, three years to the month that my marriage ended, I also ended my first serious postdivorce relationship, on the eve of the twelfth anniversary of my mother's death. It was the first year I had forgotten my mother's anniversary and one month after my divorce became official. My ex-husband, who had vowed to become a better friend the day we told my father we were splitting up, showed up when others were too fed up with my ramblings and hand-wringing over a man who had made me astoundingly unhappy for months. For some, it was not easy to understand that the sexual content of being loved, after so much loss, was simply gripping.

The sexual vulnerability so specific to postdivorce love is the very thing that rekindles your relationship to experience, but it is also what makes you that much more lonely. The dark months of summer were a time of reassessing: my commitment as a mother, my relationship to close friends, to my sexuality, and to experience itself. I let my body advance my sexual repositioning and reentry in the world. I played simple games with younger men, sexted crudely, and jumped into bed without caring one bit. I wanted the love that came from sexual vulnerability, but wanted it cheap and fast, and even though it felt bad, I preferred to feel anguish in order to maneuver around it.

Sex is never without emotional consequences. The deeper I went into a sexual relationship within my new relationship, the more the relationship drew me away from my writing, which had been, since my divorce, my center. What I gave made me realize I had no emotional self. I had a married self, a mother self, and a sexual self, but I had no "alone" self and thus no creative self.

In her process of rediscovery, Gornick turned to Dorothy Thompson, via Vincent Sheean's memoir of the pair *Dorothy and Red* ("Red" being Sinclair Lewis), just as I came to Gornick in mine. In "The Conflict Between Love and Work," also in "Essays in Feminism," she inspects their relationship and observes that Thompson, above all else, believed she needed to make herself a "creative marriage." Painfully, I read

Thompson's testimony, in her 1929 diary entry, of the life she wants. It starts out well: "What I need: more knowledge." She prizes human relationships, she wants a home, her gifts are interpretive. She's interested in humanities, politics, literature, economics, and civilized living. And then, a blow: "My passion: creative men." Gornick chalks it up to the limits of her time. Yet as needy as Thompson pretended she was, observes Gornick, she was an "unstoppable workaholic." She committed herself to as political a life as Lewis's was literary, and pretended to be helpless but carried on with life. Ironically, this most unsubmissive of women, the first reporter to get kicked out of Germany in 1934—which catapulted Thompson into fame and gave her a platform from which to publish sharp political analysis—also wrote women's interest pieces for *Ladies Home Journal*, a magazine that caters to homemakers of the most traditional kind. Is it midcentury, 1978, or 2013? In the way we mingle work and relationships, our eras seem closely intertwined. These are both the ironies and conflicts of what it means to be a woman, which feminism can merely attempt to define.

If I follow Gornick's lead, there is an argument to be made that feminism has lost steam because we've lost the ability to look at ourselves deeply. For the last decade, women have fought out a public battle in the press over whether they should work or whether they should stay at home with their children. Should they dominate or should they be submissive? We are so busy arguing with one another that we have lost the ability to recognize that perhaps we do things out of need and in time. We have also overlooked what's far more interesting: our own relationship to power. As mothers, we have tremendous power to shape our children's intellectual and emotional intelligence and to teach them how to love. And of course as women who work, think, and contribute to our culture, we grow our advantages, though perhaps more slowly. But I wonder: Do we let ourselves *feel* enough?

The incoherent dredging up Gornick talks about is so dark it is nearly unbearable. For me, it took place in the form of paining my way through, frankly, shame and undone love by writing my way out of loneliness into a place of solitude. Gornick's words brought me to the stunning recognition that I was completely alone. After the suffering it took to bring me to that realization, the relief was grand, and grounding. I was finally *in* my feet. That confident groove is a place in which you define your own clarity by digging into a tough, ever-evolving place of long-term findings. Reciting Wallace Stevens's "Sunday Morning" got me through my mother's funeral twelve years earlier. So I took to the page to transfigure the pain, the only way through it. ("Divinity must live within herself," Stevens wrote of the life of becoming.) You write, you wait. It was a truth I struggled to tolerate in grad school, in 1993. I wanted to write a certain way immediately, by working my butt off. Robert Pinsky told me that I would get to that place in time. He sighed and told me to do other things: read Ralph Ellison, see some Yiddish theater, wait.

Meanwhile, I wrote feverishly, and produced until I got married and had a child. Most women writers with children fight their inner conflict quietly and slide in a few hours when they can, and make time for what's possible. But some, like myself, just give it up. Managing a child and a household simply won out. Earlier this summer, I looked at Alix Kates Shulman's "A Marriage Agreement," which she published in 1970 in the feminist journal *Up From Under*. She asked her husband to sign the document that would guarantee her only fifty percent of the labor in raising her children. "They were always there," Shulman wrote. "I couldn't read or think. If there was ever a moment to read, I read to them." Jobs—from homework to gift-making, from transportation to sick care—would be shared fifty-fifty. I marveled. *That was 1970.* For the first three years of my son's life, I did virtually everything: I quit my job, nursed, made playdates, read to him for a half hour nightly, then coaxed him slowly to sleep. Over the course of nearly seven years, I had stopped writing, retreated from most friendships, and had become, in retrospect, an embittered zombie, walking through life and parenthood with an unease that seemed uncomfortably counter to the cheer-emoting mothers that wheeled their giant double strollers around the baby-making machine that is Park Slope.

After my divorce, a friend gave me Rachel Cusk's gutting *Aftermath: On Marriage and Separation*. She also sent me a link to her essay on Muriel Spark, in which she described the "seething muted trauma" of divorce. She was one of the few women I knew who understood the endless reeling that took place when your family was broken up and, being an expressive person, that you double-suffer not only the social and literal consequences of single parenthood but the emotional toil of working to a place of emotional balance. She took a close look at Spark's *Loitering with Intent*, and admired Spark's ability to "weave stories over an unforgiving life." And like Spark's Fleur Talbot, she too "used everyone I came across and everything I read."

Cusk was difficult to stomach. "To resist pain one must be as strong as pain, must make of oneself a kind of human bomb-shelter," she says up front. She walks around in a daze, wondering how other couples made it while she and her husband did not. The pages were a teary blur. "Everywhere people are in couples," she observes, and recalls a family trip to Agamemnon's tomb in the Peloponnese.

> Clytemnestra's tomb is there too: the two are far apart, for this is a story not of marriage but of separation, of the attempt to break the form of marriage and be free. There are two tombs, just as there were two people: separation is a demand for space, the expression of the self's need to regain its integrity.

Cusk holds nothing back and gives us her pain and the pure, cruel aftermath of a marriage ending. Eventually I stopped reading.

* * *

"The capacity to experience oneself is everything," Gornick emphasizes. The struggle to understand ourselves is about becoming human. She quotes Virginia Woolf: "Women have served all these centuries as looking-glasses possessing the magic and delicious power of reflecting the figure of man at twice its natural size." The spiritual purgatory of women, Gornick explains, is what men have depended on to produce their "maleness of experience" and thus the great works of literature that define it. So what is the "*femaleness* of experience," she asks? I've since asked myself what is my own female sensibility—and how do I articulate *that*? As I read Gornick, I feel like she's describing women now as much as the women of 1978. It's not clear whether we're any closer; perhaps it's an individual path you sort out in moments of desperation.

Gornick seemed to be describing my summer and my own unraveling: the emotional gutting of a happy divorce cleanly done, the humiliation I found myself retreading when my next relationship didn't work, the inch-by-inch fight toward self-possession from the dirty dregs. I was unable to forgive myself for my inability to contain my creative self within the confines of my marriage and of parenthood. I had also stopped writing for the entire nine-month period of my on-off romance. Because I again stopped writing, I had no internal structure. It was especially painful because for several years after my husband and I split up, I flourished creatively and wrote in new forms. That I lost myself in a relationship *again*, and an unsatisfying one at that, hit me hard.

In her essay "What Feminism Means to Me," from her 1996 collection *Approaching Eye Level*, Gornick reflects on how she married an artist and, pleased as punch with herself, thought, *Now* I can work. "Ten years later, I was wandering around New York, a divorced 'girl' of thirty-five with an aggressive style who had written a couple of articles." Then she defines the conflict that so profoundly confused me: "The lifelong inability to take myself seriously as a worker: *this* was the central dilemma of a woman's existence." (Light, music, exhilaration flowed in, Gornick said. "The slings and arrows of daily existence could not make a dent in me.") Gornick telescoped the problem in a way that helped me see that the loss of my independent self wasn't just a giving up, or just inertia, but an inability to believe. Maintaining the rhythm of my work, given that I'm a certain kind of woman, should have come first.

Gornick knows how hard it is not to prioritize a man over writing. "Loving a man, I vowed, would not again be primary." Heart-hardened and thrilled with her newfound feminist reality, she decided to settle for nothing less than "grown-up affection." Yet she recognized that "romantic love was injected like dye into the nervous system of my emotions, laced through the entire fabric of longing, fantasy, and sentiment." Even feminists want love and romance. You can't give up love, but you can be split about it. For a while, Gornick had feminism as a partner, but when feminist solidarity unraveled in 1980, she got stuck again. But she learned, just as I've been learning, that the "power over one's life comes only through the steady command of one's thought." And as she plugged away daily at her work, she found that when she thought, she was less alone. "I had myself for company," she said.

Edna in Kate Chopin's *The Awakening* didn't fare so well. She was "mesmerized" by her own spirit, Gornick says. Edna "ignores the house, forgets the children, spends hours painting, reading, thinking, walking." It was freedom or nothing. Her point of no return took place after discovering her sexual possibilities. Why sex, I keep asking myself, as I pondered the role of sexuality in becoming a more evolved woman and a more deeply feeling feminist. "Desire becomes an instrument of self-awareness," says Gornick of Edna. "Her hungers grow with inordinate speed. They become powerful, complex, demanding: and yet oddly sorrowful, tinged with a sense of foreboding." (It is true that men, confronted with the vastness of women's sexuality, reel back a bit. Just how vast is what Daniel Bergner makes clear in *What Do Women Want? Adventures in the Science of Female Desire*, along with the fact that the female eros is no better made for monogamy than the male libido.)

There it was: desire was about self-awareness, about becoming uncaged. It was a not unfortunate discovery, the years after my marriage split, that casual sex could exist in the on-and-off world of custodial parenthood. It could take place freely without the awkward recognition that a child is in the house. Sexual experience could be immersive, even obsessive, and endlessly amped up in ways that the psychological necessity of married family life would not allow. But the mistake of sexual freedom, both in my new relationship and then, later, out of it, was to assume that liberated sex corresponded to liberated emotions. Quite the opposite. The vulnerability that raw, unfettered sexual experience exposes is deepened over time, as losses accrue: the death of a parent, the tart fact of getting older, the recognition that *commitment* is a see-saw of a word that complicates and sometimes unseats actual experience.

Yet the vulnerability attached to casual sex was something to be filtered through the lens of Gornick's experiencing self. Each new sexual experience felt useful in that each party seemed to be, well, using one another, in a mutually agreed upon shared experience. This was the case with a friendly one-night stand as much as it was the case in an authentic relationship that bumbled along with tremendous uncertainty. Interestingly, once single again, I found that what men wanted was fast sex and what women wanted was to hear that I had a boyfriend, that he would move in with me, and that we would eventually marry. This is where, I started to feel, some women have failed feminism.

The face of single womanhood, to others, is often not pretty. It threatens to overwhelm other women with visions of loneliness, it undermines their self- and spouse-protecting belief that marriage is the finest and most natural denouement of a relationship, and it seems kind of slutty. Not immediately slutty, but slutty if the single lifestyle continues and settling down is not a given. Nondivorced women (let's say "nondivorced" rather than "married") initially felt titillated over my escapades and complained of their boring husbands. Every woman wants to know what it's like to have sex with a new man for the first time in a decade or so. But explaining that I would never marry again was usually greeted with silence or an overly compassionate gesture, intimating that I must be so wounded to not have faith that any man could be my second husband.

It is not always easy to explain that the very raw pain of loss is nothing if not hope-reviving. I have far more faith and curiosity about what lies ahead, in my consciousness-raising relationship to work and to other people, then I did while married. My desire is out-size. One day I may even find a man, as the ladies say. Perhaps by then I'll want one.

Churchgoing

Vespers on a Sunday afternoon.
A unified medley of a simple church
in a town on a bay where shorebirds
migrate south in autumn and oysters
hatch quietly on the shells of others.
Oystermen troll from sunset to sundown
the hard blue surface of the steady water,
decades true to it.
Old men hack at weeds with scythes
along the road that seams historic homes
and ranch houses; it stretches,
it seems, to foggy infinity.
Summer visitors leave a dollar or two
in the box up front, sign the register,
inscribe their names so they remain forever.
Old pews are polished with impeccable shine.
Opening the thick red book of Methodist hymns
in this church of every ministry,
on any Sunday, some people feel
explicit wrongs and gentle disillusionment.
The air is so clean here it feels like divinity.
I memorize the view of the old yard
behind the church, manicured and waiting.
It seems too big for anything besides flocks

of bears and horses coming in from the beach.
We are all too groomed, impeccably serious.
The pews fill up.
Women wear lipstick and honorable dresses;
men put on their Presbyterian faces.
A hunched man with a tawny ponytail
and moist eyes rises up and sobs,
"My wife is six weeks dead now."
The youngest woman in the congregation
puts her arm around him while the harpist tours
Ireland and Scotland and we all sing
Love Divine, All Loves Excelling—
I recognize the tune but not the words,
the same tune I had whispered out the window
to the sea when I was young, wondering which night
was the one the book said was silent.
And even though it wasn't mine, the song fit
then and now as the congregation
sang softly all those vowels from 1890.
I add lilt, excited to be privy to big feelings
as pastors from other towns down the peninsula,
12 of the 13 residents, the visiting minister and his wife
listen and Old Ned finishes his cry.
If love is divine then what am I

when they are so full of love
excelling? I believe in showing up.
The sermon starts.
I think about what hope is and decide it isn't
anything the minister talks about
before he's finished. Aren't we already
full of hope by coming here?
The minister tells us to question everything
so I question how he decided *wonder* was the main act
in this tiny, noble church of unseasonable reason.
I think he is saying, if we think together
without arguing about what we're thinking
we have freedom. But my wonder
is not your wonder, I think, and wonder where
he's getting all his divinity from.
These open-hearted beaches are so pure they choke me.
I prefer the cold, hard pews and visitor seating.
I prefer to be deranged and read these pretty prayers
as evil in my feet taps out a little more universe.

Dirt Maid

My tough blue hands are veined with a thousand rivers
navigated or drowned in.

But I have roots to care about, moss to take me in;
earth-maid, dirt-maid, pages of trees to grow within.

Chasing down my blue-dark conversations,
cockatoo creations, I ration thought, chase elation.

Lakes move in their reflections of trees
where light swims with full-floating ease.

A thousand years from now,
love will wonder why it ever lost its vigilance.

Perhaps: dream-crazy midnights, illicit scenes,
walking roughly into grief, casketed in it.

While stars telescope me into new geography.
Gravity climbs down trees and follows me.

River

Grooving a valley with soft-scissoring fingers,
a blind river surveys the land for a kinder ocean.
It carries the wishes of fishermen on ridges
waiting for carp to leap into their arms like a woman
and the laughter of lean sunbathers
unbothered by death that will come sooner
than they expected. Like our molecules
it aches to get to the center of earth.
It is looking for an ocean
to bury its sounds.
Stories of trilobites and volcanic heat,
birth-engine for endless microscopic species.
It moves like blood cells into impressionable soil,
tumbles over rocks,
religion truer than any.
It flows by churches,
over graveyards where we buried
star generals and tailors with musical fingers
and women who bore children
before life happened to them.
The blind river carries on its back
10-volume histories of cities that rose around them,
Tiber, Seine, Nile, Danube, Yamuna.
The river curves around new mosques

and colorful Buddhist temples with tiny flags fluttering
while Hindu deities talk about eternity.
Its mouth is our mouth, the way we shape vowels on our tongues—
It turns by a synagogue where a war-jagged rabbi
bent over his books
puzzles out what it means.
He doesn't believe in every testament.
My alphabet is weeping, he sobs.
Letters all gloss and no grace.
These words don't hold their shape.
He climbs into the waves of fresh-cut corpses
the blind river grinds to gravel,
until, many summers later,
sandbars fashion themselves into islands.
The river, sullen and implacable, is a starfish with one leg left.
It twists to a rhythm it alone hears, seeking gravity,
folk tunes in its ears and choral ghosts singing.
It plots below frozen surfaces, mineral-rich with ideas
for April, when torrential melts remind us
to everything its season.
America, colder than our hearts,
will tear us apart.
Who is courageous and what can we give up?
Small boats float on the blind river with the dead

who bicker about the price of milk and celestial news—

old stars masquerading as alive,

new stars arriving

with lightbox valises in their 200-year approach.

By then, three wars will have torn apart six countries,

a half-million men will follow their fathers into the ground.

Forests will grow blue from stem cells hidden in laboratories,

bluebells and bluebirds on their strange blossoming.

Letters to editors will be written by algorithms.

There was always too much America.

But rivers still flow in rust-belt mornings,

in algorithms propaganda can't decipher

because they are singing the sermons that unite them.

An old man, a philosopher I knew, hammers the floor with his feet,

speaking in tongues for fear of greater tragedies.

But we have long ties to sunlight that cannot be legislated,

equations that always solve for equality that is true.

The variable is us.

Intellectuals pedal bicycles fast into the wind.

There will be some yellow streamers at the end

or just a clearing where people have gathered

to dig up the wise invisible river

beneath land we have riven.

Drums and Paper

Soul, you called it,
and put on a record.
Some funk-blend

of oxygenation,
drumbeats and speed,
black doves, temples, money.

Our guttering in
between: 20 watt clairvoyance.
A decade out, we ripple

into hieroglyphs—
you interrogate my
extravagances with silence.

Sunlight's lunatic
resplendence tilts into peace.
Iridescent hills we wandered.

I spirit into blackout,
not disbelieved, *grieved*;
we live-lose daily

in drumbeats, flutes screaming
sharps and flats,
unhinging melody from its derivative.

Reverb those chords.
Lose the spectacular order
scrolling down paper.

Ankles Like Ancient Birds

I am musing for amusements,
looking for something good.

Ancestral spirits back me up.
I am searching, and they are heaven-sent.
What is beautiful? It lasts an instant.

I hand out lists of lovers and reflections.
Someone writes me a letter in seismographic beeps.
This urn, that eclipse, a nightingale, all of it true—

I despise losing but do it masterfully.
(The dead pull on my ankles like ancient birds,
my soul, they think, in reach.)

And if sea sirens and shadow-making revelations
are stage tricks? If these are standard griefs?

Sunday Morning at Queen of All Saints Church in Fort Greene

This is a place of people moving
up and down, kneeling to be supplicant
despite hymns that lift them up.
The only real motion is you.
I want to yell *hosanna*. Instead I follow you,
holding my hands out to this lord
the priest loves, and believe that he
believes. Pews are dusted with old light
the way the afternoon diffuses through ancient trees.
It is something that only happens in churches,
coaxing the sun in gothic windows
with gothic feelings of total delight,
the way a child experiences a forest,
with switchblade ferns that snap
suddenly out, and mad blossoming pink-petal eyes
warning them not to linger long
in their perilous groves of beautiful sunlight.
But we sneak fistfuls of radiance out,
something for ourselves.
That light, however little I believe, burns eternally within.
Perhaps you are more eternal than I will ever give you credit for.
The priest leads in right feeling, this feeling right
with you on this Saturday afternoon, though I had wanted
to go to the Frick and pretend I was O'Hara.

I gaze up at the stained glass windows
raised high to show me the spirit-path—
red-robed Gabriel annunciating to Mary
who smiles with uncertainty and surprise,
and wonder why angels turned up in both our stories,
why I walked through this door with you today,
your hands open to the dream of church,
and my hands, so long in my pockets, opening too.
We leave when others take communion,
with feelings so various that light follows us
and bursts into bloom on the sidewalk.
I slip my shadow into my pocket and feel,
bless you, blissful; we have stolen the swanky feelings.

With Tailfins

Down, where your questions mirror mine
but we can never reach, there is more to say about time
diminishing as we get close, in my oxygen universe.

Cold blue blur and labored breathing.
I briefly shimmered, light diffusing.

How are we to be? If I dragged you down and down,
into deep-sea serenity, love would not be coastal.

History shivers along at a thousand meters
with its tailfins and soul-seeking dinosaurs.

We are peculiar rhythm in this scuba galaxy,
all dark dreams below waves that always crumble.

It is not enough to see the edges of eternity.
We dive recklessly for stingrays, swordfish, anemones.

Down and down, where the question is pure belief
not clarity, I bring you to this rendezvous with me.
I reach my hand into sun-shattering darkness, then pull it free.

Aphrodisiac Drift

Summer of bonfires in which I go swimming,
Spirit-animating breezes on which I am living
In formidable arrangements of bliss and despair,
Durably plural. I never promised I could fix it,
Derek, the mistakability of poems, words shuffling
In my head. It is midsummer again, with its steam-blaze
Atlantic sea-light and its fanatic infusions of sweet
Loss, its syllables inevitable. Make it rhythm, you said.
Your advice gave me twenty years of aphrodisiac drift.
I am swimming in the bonfire of summer in Brooklyn,
Barking at enchantments and climbing in caskets
I've loved. I've mapped a witch hunt for myself.
My crimes are too tiny and too interior to matter much.
I am a walking-awkward vernacular specific to myself.

Fog Trench

A sea-gap opens as surf crumbles
onto shifting sediment that pretends to be a beach
but has the bones of 13,000 years;
quartz blades and sea otter pelts, the fur-trade
driving settlements that would commence
the New World with its shipyards and apple orchards,
wheat fields newly immortal in the summer winds
erupting into lumber, salmon, smelters
for goldfields. Then come the wars
with accurate brutalities that spawn the local skill
of finding ways within the wind so aerodynamic
you'd think the jets would get to heaven first—
But I have found a shortcut on the beach,
a little ladder with infinite depth
from the moon that shimmers
on this cool night, crepuscular and orange,
to the plum-black ocean trenches
where only fang-tooths dare to wander.
Those sideways stairs cut into waves
are momentarily distinct before they splinter
into a million strobes of light
as if a million stars were reflected in them.
My old bones shiver.
I am strides away from 30,000 feet.

The stairs close in, the ocean ebbs,
they form again, forever scrambling into place.
A boat comes in, glinting with its sea-light
as if trying to tell us something spectacular.
They were never holy, these local stairs,
as much as knowledge-deepening,
sweetening the commerce, home, and love we toil for
here, before we climb to galaxies offshore
on these dissolving stairs that are no more.

Tabernacles Will Turn to Sieves

In my house of rooms
I measure what can't be left or gotten over.
Lowercase letters climb up and down stairways,
bedrooms crumble inside a million broken mirrors,
foyers are lined with birthday cake.

Marching bands accompany me
to the daily precipice.

Effigies of old women give away papers
scribbled with tricks that seem transgressive.
Gods that are not god to anybody.
The love of a second god, or a third that shadows it.
Or shadows themselves, truths to grudgingly love
though it doesn't burn like some tree
and it feels kind of frozen.

I was a fool to put my hand in.
Your tabernacles will turn to sieves, it said.

So I open my briefcase of balms and correctives
and stack them in cupboards of my ancient house.
I welcome the gladiators and mermaids
who are there to murder me.

Let them do it. I will decorate this house
with the future tense. I fill my house with hymns.

Forest with Castanets

Lightning on a sunlit day,
heaven-bright sparrows fly into shade
so momentarily dark I lose my bearings.

The purest glow has the whitest dazzle.
It will burn your cheeks off.

Listen, it will make your bones stars again.
Give me a mystery to count on.
Turn me inside out; heart, bones, tendons,
all the facts to make a proper woman of.

I sound lovelier than I will ever be,
beyond annunciations, above altars of belief.
Nosing through glitter, I record everything I see.

*

Along the uninhabited edge
below fear-freaked storms and near-sound
my gray ash lifts, determined to make sense.

All one thing, this heaven-scaffold on a beach,
promising phosphorescence.

Someone has laid out a red carpet:
Blood-feathers on a sandy graveyard.
A bald eagle tracking its kill magnificently loses.
(Was he the murderer, you wonder.)

I am the only one here.
Am I an optical trick between air and sea?
My ankles ache to be certain.

*

Unshoe my feet and let them pirouette
their proclamations. They yield to nothing.
They are savagely precise.

They freefall naturally
to rhythms learned and steps incorrigible.

That groove is too much with me.
I throw my arms up,
legs out, hips around, and ramble on.
My heartbeat steals each breath,
I stomp and stomp.
If I could see inside an owl's beak

I'd find nothing newer than the primitive.
What's far-flung is the repetitive, quietly thumping beat
uncertain of its own very dangerous feet.

2

I am racing through forest where clouds,
already in the light, are burning off.
Pale pink light sharpens the foothills.

Oh, to be *that* keen
for an act so ordinary.

Roots of roots, the etymological slur:
slugs, maggots, moss, and inner fruitfulness.
Who will I meet, pinecones in my ears
and digging for mist that was heaven-sent?

A drop of dew, concave with despondencies of world
and my reflections. It adds up, the *that*
which sticks despite confusion and illusion
when our bones break loose for no reason.

*

Rambling, perfect grooves on a maple's trunk,
fat leaves leaping into bags we raked and raked.

Our fingernails grew black with soft soil,
soil I'll put you into, and where you'll wait for me.

The maple is my stairway up. I climb on it forever.

The tallest branches bend under my weight.
Built for disaster, they yield but don't break.

*

Glamour of old books and operatic eyes
linger in this galaxy where years rise
but seem lateral, too brief to define what losing is.

Perhaps we master it but find little.
The sun is ablaze and dead souls scratch at the years.

What I learned, and what consoles:
Here is the orchestra and the men who play horns,
here's how the conductor moves things along.
Here are the women who teach me to sew

all that seems seamless, to mend as we grow.

It is not the rhythm I expected.
Perhaps it is better to correct it.

Years tumble by. Kind people from dead times
shake their castanets and hand me their rhymes.

The Organized Magic of My Father

Better than belief is hand-cranked science
you raised me with; dreams you rearranged
and solved for x. Faith's no proof, you said.

Yet moving through the silence of somber adulations
souls slide into churning constellations,
they find new fates and new enchantments.

Your organized magic shifts my narrative of cloud-drift;
in every direction you place symbols, fomulas, notations.

These dreams you wondered over, waited for
are starkly lit. They whisper: What is your ultimate belief
in this last life, what will you leave me with?

Pure chemicals dissolve to pure belief.
The body is soulful in the science of what it ends with.

Between the Beats

Eyelashes flicker, heedful of my presence
in his half-shadow light.
His eyes will grow darker and more substantial
solving for x equations of love, only yet
still mine alone to ponder, but in five years,
sooner than he thinks, he will have hazarded,
briefly, grief, between reciprocal
commonplace cadences of falling for someone.
His legs will grow long-limbed, he will become
a birch tree climbing out of himself
into youth-new hues of wild
impressionistic sky: what is refracted
in his eyes the way he wants to see it.
This is how time passes,
in your own loop of whirl.
Life is as easy as you make it, I tell him,
but don't count on anything but experience
and us. The rest is real only in philosophy,
cosmic forks and knives clashing,
not rhythm in your feet.
By then he will be drafted, at 18, into brutalities of men,
into oil-hungry strategies of firepower and defense.
Sign here to kill cinnamon faces born elsewhere
according to fine-tuned small lettering.

Here is your government-issued machete.

Sign here for your blood-blue rules, your green money.

Or instead the war will be interior.

He will ache for fast love too fast to notice it has faded.

Slower love finds its voice in conversations of sparrows.

Even now he is a bowerbird

collecting pretty ideas as he builds his nest

away from me.

I created his heart, kidneys, fingerprints, lungs, eyes.

I put my molecules in his mind.

I pause in the gears of age

and look at my list. Notice, I instruct, the plane

approach its runway with beautiful uncertainty,

the mechanical angle of wings as the pilot

pulls gently back, hovering.

His feet hit the ground, racing to the next thing.

He is a half-composed time-tricking riff.

Drums find their best rhythm between the beats,

he tells me and I agree. Love always backflips into your life,

I offer, but he is skeptical at 13.

Which is worse, he asks, death or heartbreak?

I shrug and say only heartbreak ends,

for the living. I point to bookshelves.

Despair fits neatly into verbs and you can make them bubble

just like love, I say, reluctant to say that fizz is a property of time
but verbs sit on the page forever.
The mind at its fastest and most vulnerable
sees lost sentences only you can find.
Sometimes they are invisible
like origami in your soul,
an unfolding folded-up feeling of chaos and design.
When you become a man, an invented thing,
believe me it is something unusual,
that approach to genuine feelings, that hovering.

Acknowledgments:

Bellevue Press, The Common, Guernica, How to Write Poetry (Barnes & Noble Books, 2005), The Literary Review, Notre Dame Review, The Paris Review Daily, Prairie Schooner, Red Hen Anthology of Contemporary Indian Writing (Red Hen Press, 2019), Stonecutter, Slate, Subtropics, and *Salamander.*

Thanks to Minna Proctor, Robert Pinsky, Derek Walcott, Bill Matthews, Kwame Dawes, Martha Rhodes, Ryan Murphy, Michael Morse, Edwin Frank, Lyn DiIorio, René Steinke, Sudeep Sen, Lynn Melnick, Brigid Hughes, Nina Mehta, James Marcus, Jerry Sticker, Tom Russell, Ivan Russell, my dad Dilip Mehta, and in memory of my mother Carole Leonard. My grateful appreciation to Dorset Colony and Wilapa Bay AiR for giving me time, support, and space to write.

Born in Frankfurt, Germany, and raised in Bombay and New Jersey, Diane Mehta studied with Derek Walcott and Robert Pinsky in the nineties and has been an editor at PEN America's *Glossolalia, Guernica,* and *A Public Space.* Her book about writing poetry was published by Barnes & Noble Books in 2005. She lives in Brooklyn, New York.

Publication of this book was made possible by grants and donations. We are also grateful to those individuals who participated in our 2018 Build a Book Program. They are:

Anonymous (11), Sally Ball, Vincent Bell, Jan Bender-Zanoni, Kristina Bicher, Laurel Blossom, Adam Bohanon, Betsy Bonner, Mary Brancaccio, Lee Briccetti, Jane Martha Brox, Carla & Steven Carlson, Caroline Carlson, Stephanie Chang, Tina Chang, Liza Charlesworth, Andrea Cohen, Machi Davis, Marjorie Deninger, Patrick Donnelly, Charles Douthat, Emily Flitter, Lukas Fauset, Monica Ferrell, Jennifer Franklin, Helen Fremont & Donna Thagard, Robert Fuentes & Martha Webster, Ryan George, Panio Gianopoulos, Chuck Gillett, Lauri Grossman, Julia Guez, Naomi Guttman & Jonathan Mead, Steven Haas, Lori Hauser, Mary & John Heilner, Ricardo Hernandez, Deming Holleran, Nathaniel Hutner, Janet Jackson, Rebecca Kaiser Gibson, David Lee, Jen Levitt, Howard Levy, Owen Lewis, Sara London & Dean Albarelli, David Long, Katie Longofono, Cynthia Lowen, Ralph & Mary Ann Lowen, Jacquelyn Malone, Fred Marchant, Donna Masini, Catherine McArthur, Nathan McClain, Richard McCormick, Victoria McCoy, Britt Melewski, Kamilah Moon, Beth Morris, Rebecca Okrent, Gregory Pardlo, Veronica Patterson, Jill Pearlman, Marcia & Chris Pelletiere, Maya Pindyck, Megan Pinto, Taylor Pitts, Eileen Pollack, Barbara Preminger, Kevin Prufer, Vinode Ramgopal, Martha Rhodes, Peter & Jill Schireson, Jason Schneiderman, Jane Scovel, Andrew Seligsohn & Martina Anderson, Soraya Shalforoosh, James Snyder & Krista Fragos, Ann St. Claire, Alice St. Claire-Long, Dorothy Tapper Goldman, Robin Taylor, Marjorie & Lew Tesser, Boris Thomas, Judith Thurman, Susan Walton, Calvin Wei, Bill Wenthe, Allison Benis White, Elizabeth Whittlesey, Rachel Wolff, Hao Wu, Anton Yakovlev, and Leah Zander.